P9-CBC-435

Acts 1-12
God Moves
in the Early Church

CHUCK AND WINNIE
CHRISTENSEN

FISHERMAN
BIBLE STUDYGUIDES

Acts 1–12

PUBLISHED BY WATERBROOK PRESS

12265 Oracle Boulevard, Suite 200

Colorado Springs, Colorado 80921

Scripture taken from the *Holy Bible, New International Version*®. NIV®. Copyright © 1973, 1978, 1984 by International Bible Society. Used by permission of Zondervan Publishing House. All rights reserved.

ISBN 978-0-87788-007-3

Copyright © 1979, revised editions 1993, 2005 by Chuck and Winnie Christensen

All rights reserved. No part of this book may be reproduced or transmitted in any form or by any means, electronic or mechanical, including photocopying and recording, or by any information storage and retrieval system, without permission in writing from the publisher.

Published in the United States by WaterBrook Multnomah, an imprint of the Crown Publishing Group, a division of Random House Inc., New York.

Printed in the United States of America

2010

10 9 8 7 6 5 4

Contents

How to Use This Studyguide

*F*isherman studyguides are based on the inductive approach to Bible study. Inductive study is discovery study; we discover what the Bible says as we ask questions about its content and search for answers. This is quite different from the process in which a teacher *tells* a group *about* the Bible—what it means and what to do about it. In inductive study, God speaks directly to each of us through his Word.

A group functions best when a leader keeps the discussion on target, but the leader is neither the teacher nor the "answer person." A leader's responsibility is to *ask*—not *tell.* The answers come from the text itself as group members examine, discuss, and think together about the passage.

There are four kinds of questions in each study. The first is an *approach question.* Asked and answered before the Bible passage is read, this question breaks the ice and helps you start thinking about the topic of the Bible study. It begins to reveal where thoughts and feelings need to be transformed by Scripture.

Some of the earlier questions in each study are *observation questions*—who, what, where, when, and how—designed to help you learn some basic facts about the passage of Scripture.

Once you know what the Bible says, you need to ask, *What does it mean?* These *interpretation questions* help you discover the writer's basic message.

Next come *application questions,* which ask, *What does it mean to me?* They challenge you to live out the Scripture's life-transforming message.

Fisherman studyguides provide spaces between questions for jotting down responses as well as any related questions you would like to raise in the group. Each group member should have a copy of the studyguide and may take a turn in leading the group.

A group should use any accurate, modern translation of the Bible such as the *New International Version,* the *New American Standard Bible,* the *New Living Translation,* the *New Revised Standard Version,* the *New Jerusalem Bible,* or the *Good News Bible.* (Other translations or paraphrases of the Bible may be referred to when additional help is needed.) Bible commentaries should not be brought to a Bible study because they tend to dampen discussion and keep people from thinking for themselves.

SUGGESTIONS FOR GROUP LEADERS

1. Thoroughly read and study the Bible passage before the meeting. Get a firm grasp on its themes and begin applying its teachings for yourself. Pray that the Holy Spirit will "guide you into all truth" (John 16:13) so that your leadership will guide others.

2. If any of the studyguide's questions seem ambiguous or unnatural to you, rephrase them, feeling free to add others that seem necessary to bring out the meaning of a verse.

3. Begin (and end) the study promptly. Start by asking someone to pray that every participant will both understand the passage and be open to its transforming power. Remember, the Holy Spirit is the teacher, not you!

4. Ask for volunteers to read the passages aloud.

5. As you ask the studyguide's questions in sequence, encourage everyone to participate in the discussion. If some are silent, try gently suggesting, "Let's have an answer from someone who hasn't spoken up yet."

6. If a question comes up that you can't answer, don't be afraid to admit that you're baffled. Assign the topic as a research project for someone to report on next week, or say, "I'll do some studying and let you know what I find out."

7. Keep the discussion moving, but be sure it stays focused. Though a certain number of tangents are inevitable, you'll want to quickly bring the discussion back to the topic at hand. Also, learn to pace the discussion so that you finish the lesson in the time allotted.

8. Don't be afraid of silences; some questions take time to answer, and some people need time to gather courage to speak. If silence persists, rephrase your question, but resist the temptation to answer it yourself.

9. If someone comes up with an answer that is clearly illogical or unbiblical, ask for further clarification: "What verse suggests that to you?"

10. Discourage overuse of cross references. Learn all you can from the passage at hand, while selectively incorporating a few important references suggested in the studyguide.

11. Some questions are marked with a ✐. This indicates that further information is available in the Leader's Notes at the back of the guide.

12. For more information on getting a new Bible study group started and keeping it functioning effectively, read *You Can Start a Bible Study Group* by Gladys M. Hunt and *Pilgrims in Progress: Growing Through Groups* by Jim and Carol Plueddemann. (Both books are available from Shaw Books.)

Suggestions for Group Members

1. Learn and apply the following ground rules for effective Bible study. (If new members join the group later, review these guidelines with the whole group.)

2. Remember that your goal is to learn all you can *from the Bible passage being studied.* Let it speak for itself without using Bible commentaries or other Bible passages. There is more than enough in each assigned passage to keep your group productively occupied for one session. Sticking to the passage saves the group from insecurity ("I don't have the right reference books—or the time to read anything else.") and confusion ("Where did *that* come from? I thought we were studying _____.").

3. Avoid the temptation to bring up those fascinating tangents that don't really grow out of the passage you are discussing. If the topic is of common interest, you can bring it up later in informal conversation after the study. Meanwhile, help one another stick to the subject.

4. Encourage one another to participate. People remember best what they discover and verbalize for

themselves. Some people are naturally shy, while others may be afraid of making a mistake. If your discussion is free and friendly and you show real interest in what other group members think and feel, the quieter ones will be more likely to speak up. Remember, the more people involved in a discussion, the richer it will be.

5. Guard yourself from answering too many questions or talking too much. Give others a chance to share their ideas. If you are one who participates easily, discipline yourself by counting to ten before you open your mouth.

6. Make personal, honest applications and commit yourself to letting God's Word change you.

Introduction

Whenever a new movement gains momentum, we ask basic questions about it. How did it start? What were the obstacles? Who was associated with it? What is its present condition? Where is it going? The early chapters of the book of Acts answer these questions about the church of Jesus Christ. The following general outline provides an overview of the action.

In Acts 1 and 2 we discover the church's beginnings when the disciples were bound together by the coming of the Holy Spirit from heaven. With his baptism, they received power to be witnesses of the life, death, and resurrection of Jesus Christ.

Acts 3 through 8 tell us of believers preaching with power a message of forgiveness for sins and reconciliation to God. The message and its repercussions filled Jerusalem. Opposition developed. The established Jewish leaders tried to snuff out this new and growing movement.

In Acts 9 through 12 we find that stamping out the church was no more successful than stamping on mercury! Persecution only scattered and spread the believers; consequently, the Christian witness caught hold more rapidly throughout Judea and Samaria. When the church's chief enemy Saul (Paul) became a follower of Christ, the church was finally allowed to grow and develop unhindered.

The writer of the book of Acts was Luke, a medical doctor. His sources were the early disciples. He interviewed them on dusty trails, aboard ship, and in prison houses. He had previously written a gospel, and he felt a responsibility to accurately record the events in the life of the early church. This is not a complete history of all that happened in the middle of the first century, but by the Spirit of God, Luke recorded clear, foundational facts about the church.

When the church began, all its members were Jews. Luke tells us how the Gentiles were joined to them in fellowship. He established the fact that Christianity was a religion separate from Judaism, drawing together people of many racial and religious backgrounds.

The early church was confined to Judea, a small country at the eastern end of the Mediterranean. By the time the first generation of Christians had blended into the next, the message was spreading to remote corners of the Roman Empire.

Luke laid out a pattern for local church life: a community of joyful believers, empowered by the Spirit, living for the Lord and one another, concerned about sharing with others the joy and reinforcement of their circle of fellowship. The believers tasted persecution and saw God miraculously protect them. Supernatural signs and wonders were part of their daily lives. Assaults from enemies within and without were met with courage and wisdom from God. The Lord was moving among them!

Be alert as you study. You'll become intrigued and involved. This new, growing movement that Luke described, with its powerful message as well as its problems, reminds us of our world today and of its need for a message from God. Praise God, the Holy Spirit is just as active now, as he was then, to convert, strengthen, and preserve all those who believe in Jesus Christ. God is moving among us, too!

A PROMISED GIFT

ACTS 1

*F*our-year-old Denise had walked up and down these steps to her Sunday-school class many times before. They were steep, and Mom always held her hand. But one day after Sunday school was over, Denise looked up into the face of the woman whose hand had tightly gripped hers as they walked downstairs to church—and it wasn't Mom's face! Here was one four-year-old who wanted some answers, and quickly! Her cries could be heard all the way up the stairwell.

Each of us has experienced the temporary or more long-lasting loss of people in our lives. We watch family members, favorite teachers, pastors, and friends move away. We know that other people will eventually fill the now-empty role, but the emotional adjustment is a significant one for us.

We can imagine how lost the disciples felt when the risen Jesus drifted up and out of their reach. Their only comfort was the promise he had made: He would not leave them alone.

1. Describe a time when someone you loved had to leave you. How did you feel?

READ ACTS 1:1-5.

2. What kind of communication did Jesus have with his followers after his resurrection? Why was it important for the disciples to be convinced that his resurrection was true and real?

3. What were Jesus's followers to wait for?

READ ACTS 1:6-11.

4. What kind of kingdom were the disciples concerned about (verse 6)? What was Jesus's concern (verses 7-8)?

5. Picture yourself as one of Jesus's disciples. What feelings and thoughts would you have had as Jesus left

Indicates further information in Leader's Notes

you? With what promise did the angels bring the disciples back to reality?

READ ACTS 1:12-26.

6. Who was missing from the group of disciples? How did the Eleven spend their time (verse 14)?

7. According to verse 15, how much had the group of believers grown? Who became their spokesman? What deliberate choice had Judas made in spite of the same exposure to Jesus that the other eleven disciples had experienced?

✐ 8. What specific qualifications were necessary for Judas's successor (verses 21-22)? What part did the group play in this choice? Read Proverbs 16:33 to see how God can use "chance" to reveal his will.

9. Note the pattern of obedience, expectancy, and prayer that characterized the believers. Which of these are part of your life? If any of these qualities are not a regular part of your life, what practical steps can you take to incorporate them?

Pray together, asking God to give you a growing faith.

The Gift
Is Given

Acts 2:1-21

The young short-term missionary was beginning to understand Arabic, but the requests being voiced in this prayer meeting were still far beyond her comprehension. And she needed real prayer tonight: Back in the States, her father had developed serious complications with his diabetes. Hesitantly, she raised her hand and made a halting request for him, using "baby Arabic" as she called it. It was the least she could do.

But a few moments later, when the strange language rose and fell all around her, two familiar words jumped out at her— her name and the word meaning "father." The voices rose with more urgency, and tears stung at the missionary's eyes. She knew—she *sensed*—that her sick father was receiving the most beautiful prayer that faith could offer. She marveled at how the Holy Spirit could unite hearts and needs in such a diversity of sounds, words, and meanings.

This second chapter in the book of Acts gives the amazing account of the Holy Spirit's first miraculous appearance among the believers of the early church.

1. Is it easy or difficult for you to learn a foreign language? What would motivate you to learn another language?

READ ACTS 2:1-13.

2. Imagine yourself as one of the disciples, quietly praying with other believers in a home. In your own words, describe the startling things you would have heard and seen (verses 2-4).

3. According to verse 4, what promise was being kept (see Acts 1:4-5)? How many of the believers were filled with the Spirit? What special supernatural ability did the Holy Spirit give these believers?

4. What brought the huge, cosmopolitan crowd together in front of the place where the believers were
   praying (verse 6)? What amazed them (verses 6-8)?

5. What was the common topic of all the messages in
   the various languages? What "wonders of God" had
   the speakers recently witnessed? What was the reaction of some in the crowd (verse 13)?

READ ACTS 2:14-21.

6. According to Peter's explanation of the phenomenon
   described in verses 6-11, what was it *not?* What,
   then, was it (verse 16-21)?

7. Upon whom did Joel predict the Spirit would be
   poured (verse 17)? What results would follow this
   outpouring?

8. Which part of Joel's prophecy began to be fulfilled right then? Which part is still a future event?

9. What invitation does the Holy Spirit extend to all people in every generation (verse 21)? What does it mean to be saved? Have you called on the Lord's name for salvation? If not, why not?

PETER'S PLEA

ACTS 2:22-47

We never know the effect our words will have. Years after a conversation, someone reminds us of something funny or wise—or hurtful—we said, something we likely don't even remember saying. At times we feel that no one listens when we say something of importance; on other occasions we are suddenly aware that we have a sizable audience, and the room has grown still in anticipation of what we are about to say. It can be a flattering and frightening experience.

On the Day of Pentecost, amid the "confusion" of so many languages being spoken at once, Peter found himself surrounded by a great many people who wanted to know what was going on. He probably looked around, wondering who would calm them down. Before, Jesus had always handled these situations. But Jesus wasn't with them anymore. It was all up to the disciples. No—not only them. The Holy Spirit was upon them, and Peter knew what he must do.

1. What is the most memorable speech or sermon you've heard? What made it so memorable?

Read Acts 2:22-36.

2. Who now becomes the central focus of Peter's message? List all the ways God the Father was involved in the life and works of Jesus, his Son (verses 22-36).

3. To whom did Peter clearly assign responsibility for Jesus's death? Why was it impossible for death to hold Jesus? What made him different from all other human beings? (See 1 Peter 2:22; 3:18.)

4. What historical event had David foreseen and written about in the psalm Peter quoted (verse 31)? How did Peter re-emphasize the reality of this event?

5. What is the relationship between Jesus's current position and the outpouring of the Holy Spirit (verse 33)?

6. What two facts about Jesus do all Jews (and all other people) need to know beyond a shadow of a doubt (verse 36)?

Read Acts 2:37-47.

7. What effect did Peter's sermon have on his listeners? What did their question reveal about them? What is the first essential action in Peter's reply to them? Using a dictionary and your own experience, define the verb *repent*.

8. How would the people have felt when they heard they could be forgiven, even after crucifying Jesus? What does *forgiven* mean to you?

9. Who is included in the promise in verse 39? How does this promise apply to us today?

10. How did the listeners respond to Peter's clear-cut instructions? What four activities did the new believers devote themselves to (verse 42)? Why are these activities important for all Christians?

11. How did the people react to the events (verse 43)?
What characteristic of this group of believers would
draw others to them?

12. Based on verses 44-47, what are some practical ways
believers today can show their love and care for one
another? How is the Lord involved in our growth as
a church and as individuals (verse 47)?

13. Briefly review the events and the spoken words in
this chapter. What clues do you find as to how God
the Holy Spirit wants to work in your life today?

JUMPING FOR JOY

ACTS 3

*M*ost of us have known someone who developed spiritual hunger during an illness. Being reminded of the body's frailty often opens a door to the deeper questions of emotional and spiritual need.

But when Peter healed the beggar in Jesus's name, the man was not expecting anything of a spiritual nature; he was too caught up in his physical suffering to visualize anything beyond a handout. After he was healed, he jumped for joy, but chances are he would not make spiritual connections on his own.

Neither would the crowd. As far as they were concerned, a miracle had happened for no apparent reason. Peter decided that remaining silent would allow error to enter into the minds of the man and those who had witnessed his healing. Sometimes God's people must be interpreters of God's actions in the world.

1. How do you react when someone asks you for money?

READ ACTS 3:1-10.

2. How long had the man been lame? By whose authority did Peter speak and act? What was the result (verses 7-8)?

3. What verbs show the healed man's physical and emotional response? What had he asked for? What did he get? How could his healing change the whole pattern of his life?

∅ 4. What was the reaction of the people in the temple? How would this miracle substantiate the apostles' message?

READ ACTS 3:11-16.

5. To whom did Peter turn the crowd's attention? What had the God of the patriarchs (whom they revered) done for Jesus? What had the people done with Jesus?

6. What did it take for Christ's power to be effective in the lame man's life? How did Peter describe the man who had been healed?

READ ACTS 3:17-26.

7. What did Peter recognize about the motivation of those who killed Jesus? What remedy for past sin is given in verse 19? What would this message mean for those in Peter's audience who had participated in Jesus's death?

8. Where is Jesus today (verse 21)? What is he waiting for?

9. Who was the "prophet" (verse 22) and the "servant" (verse 26)? Who else foretold these events?

10. According to verses 19-26, what are the benefits of listening to God through Jesus and the prophets. What happens to those who do not listen?

As you consciously listen to God's voice this week, remember to obey what he says. Next week, come prepared to share how he has blessed you.

A PRAYER FOR
BOLDNESS

ACT 4:1-31

*H*eather couldn't believe this was happening. Professor Connely was seating himself at the lunch table with Heather and some other students. He was a brilliant, charming man, although it had been a great disappointment to hear him speak of Christianity in disparaging terms last week during class. But this was a nice chance to socialize.

It felt wonderful until Aaron, a classmate and new Christian, brought up the resurrection of Jesus. A disgruntled look came into Professor Connely's eyes. Heather had done a lot of studying on the resurrection—the proofs and the arguments. Any other time she would have charged into the conversation, helping Aaron present the evidence. But the professor's look of disapproval was enough to turn her into a meek person who merely smiled noncommittally.

Most Christians can relate to Heather's experience. But most of us have never had to deal with the kind of pressure that the disciples faced in Acts 4.

1. When do you tend to feel most intimidated? Speaking in front of a large crowd? Interviewing for a job? Going on a first date? Why?

READ ACTS 4:1-12.

∂ 2. Why would Peter's teaching have threatened the religious leaders? How did the leaders respond to Peter's words?

3. After arresting Peter and John, the Jewish leaders interrogated them. What was their question? What was Peter's source of strength when he responded? How did this experience fulfill the promise Jesus gave the disciples in Mark 13:11?

4. Peter likened the religious leaders to builders (verse 11). Of what did he accuse them? What had happened to the rejected capstone? (See Psalm 118:22-23.)

5. What exclusive statement did Peter make about Jesus Christ (verse 12)? Who is included in "we"? Why did this group of religious leaders need to be saved?

READ ACTS 4:13-22.

6. What qualities in Peter and John impressed the Sanhedrin? To what did the religious leaders attribute Peter and John's confidence?

7. What was the council's dilemma? What did they attempt to prevent? Who was the ultimate authority for Peter and John?

Read Acts 4:23-31.

⟋ 8. In their prayer, what did the local believers acknowledge about God's power? Having reminded themselves of God's power and purposes, what request did the believers make (verses 29-30)? How did God answer their prayer?

9. What had David predicted about the response of nations and their rulers to Jesus Christ (verses 25-26)? How had the recent events in Jerusalem fulfilled God's plan (verse 28)?

10. To whom do you need to speak God's Word boldly? Ask God to show you his greatness and give you courage to witness for him.

SHARING POSSESSIONS

ACTS 4:32–5:11

*N*umerous communal-living situations have cropped up in recent and not-so-recent history. Some have been religious orders; others have been havens for "free love" and minimal individual responsibility. Still others have been more politically oriented—endeavoring to live out community in a nonmaterialistic and egalitarian way.

Followers of Jesus who were living in or visiting Jerusalem at the time of Pentecost had unique needs and opportunities. The community they formed during this exciting time has given modern-day church communities much to think about.

1. What kinds of resources are easy for you to share with others? What kinds of things are hard for you to share? Explain.

READ ACTS 4:32-37.

2. How did the believers in the developing church express their oneness? What was their attitude toward material possessions?

3. How did the believers' unity affect their witness to others? What was the central theme of their message?

4. Several facts are given about Joseph in verses 36 and 37. What does each element of this description add to our understanding of him?

READ ACTS 5:1-11.

5. Contrast Barnabas's attitudes and actions with those of Ananias and Sapphira. What supernatural power was moving in each?

6. Whom did Ananias and Sapphira think they were deceiving (verse 2)? To whom were they actually lying (verse 4)?

7. How and why do people today give false impressions?

8. What true reply could Sapphira have given to Peter's question in verse 8?

9. What was the reaction of the church to the couple's death? Why was it necessary for the young church to learn this difficult lesson?

10. How serious is it when Christians pretend to "surrender all" to God but deliberately hold back from him? How important is truth to God? (See Psalm 51:6.)

11. If someone were to describe your local church today, which of the terms used to describe the believers in Acts 4 would apply? What elements are missing, if any? What do you need so that you can contribute to the power, unity, outreaching love, and witness of your local church?

GOD'S WORK

ACTS 5:12-42

A recent issue of *Christianity Today* magazine carried several articles about present-day Christians who are suffering for their faith. In some places it is still a capital offense to believe in Jesus. In other situations it is not the belief itself, but rather the principles a believer stands for—principles that threaten certain political agendas—that land many Christians in jail, torture chambers, or exile.

The believers in the book of Acts were Jews living under Roman rule. But in matters of daily life and faith, they answered to a tightly woven, ethnic religious system. In Acts 5, it is religious—not political or military—leaders who test the faithfulness of the young church.

1. How do you think you would react if you were sent to jail because of your beliefs?

READ ACTS 5:12-16.

2. The Christians met on Solomon's Colonnade, a section of the temple area. What did the general public think of these followers of Christ?

3. What supernatural powers did the apostles exercise? How effective was their ministry?

READ ACTS 5:17-32.

4. What motivated the religious leaders to arrest the apostles? For what purpose were they miraculously set free? How would this miracle help them to be bold in the future?

5. What accusation did the high priest make (verse 28)? When had a similar charge been made? Why might the high priest have had a guilty conscience?

6. What principle dictated the apostles' decisions?

7. How had the Jews responded to their promised Savior (verse 30)? How was God's grace still being extended to them?

READ ACTS 5:33-42.

8. Why did Peter's statement enrage the religious leaders? Who quieted them with his logic? Why would the other members of the council listen to him?

9. What advice did Gamaliel give to the council? What did he realize about God's work?

✐ 10. In response to Gamaliel's advice, what did the council do to the apostles? What was the apostles' reaction to such pressure?

11. The apostles' constant response to hostile pressure was one of courage, joy, and loyalty to Jesus. What made them different from the kind of men they were before Jesus's crucifixion?

12. Are you experiencing the power of the Spirit filling and changing you? Explain. If your answer is no, you will want to follow the believers' example in Acts 1:14 and 4:31.

CARING CHRISTIANS

ACTS 6

*I*n some ways, present-day churches have adapted them-selves to business models of operation rather than ministry models. Young pastors build up their own credentials at small, less wealthy churches so that they can move on to larger and more prestigious ones. Titles after a name become important, as well as the size of a person's office space—and paycheck.

The outward characteristics of the early church commu-nity were quite different, but the apostles had to make deci-sions early on regarding the division of responsibility and the logistics of maintaining a fair and loving community.

1. Which jobs in your church are the hardest to find volunteers for? Why do you think this is the case?

READ ACTS 6:1-7.

2. What problem arose as the church grew in size? What system for mutual provision had already been established in the church? (See Acts 2:44-45.)

3. What did the apostles recognize as *their* main responsibility (verses 2-4)? What specific qualifications were necessary for their helpers? Why?

4. In what ways do Christians in the church serve each other today as these deacons did? (See also 1 Timothy 3:8-13.)

⌀ 5. How did the body of Christians react to the apostles'
request? How were the men commissioned for their
new responsibility?

6. Once the church's internal inconsistencies were
addressed, to what extent was the effectiveness of the
gospel message increased (verse 7)? What religious
group was reached? What had been this group's
response until now? (See Acts 4:1-2 and 5:17.)

7. Bearing in mind the results of Christians caring for
one another's needs, how do you think your local
church could increase the effectiveness of its outreach
in the community? What could you do personally?

READ ACTS 6:8-15.

8. Aside from caring for the Grecian widows in the
church, what special events marked Stephen's

ministry (verse 8)? Describe Stephen, using the information about him in verses 5, 8, 10, and 15. Now describe him as he was seen by his opponents.

9. Why were the arguments against Stephen ineffective? What tactic did his accusers resort to? What did this reveal about them?

10. Compare yourself with Stephen. Which of his characteristics are present or lacking in your life and ministry? Explain. Ask God to fill you with his "grace and power" (verse 8).

STEPHEN'S SPEECH

ACTS 7:1-53

*I*n recent years, a number of books have been written to retell history by including the viewpoints of people whose voices have not been heard adequately in the past. Thus, we have history told from the perspectives of women, African Americans, American Indians, indigenous peoples of Latin America, and so on. For people to feel included in the world, they must see their heritages represented and be reminded of who they are.

When deacon Stephen gave the speech in Acts 7, he was retelling the history of Israel from God's point of view—reminding his listeners of who they were and what their responsibilities were before an almighty and loving God.

1. What type of history do you find most interesting? World history? Church history? Your family history? Explain.

READ ACTS 7:1-53.

2. Look at the conclusion of Stephen's speech (verses 51-53). How did he describe the Israelites' ancestors? What was their response to God's messengers and to the law? Keep these conclusions in mind as you discuss the rest of the chapter.

3. As he stood before the Jewish council, Stephen summarized Israel's history, telling them what God had done for Abraham and his descendants. What promises did God make? What difficulties did he predict?

4. What did God do *for* Joseph and later *through* him?

5. According to verses 17-22, what danger arose for the nation of Israel? Who became God's messenger? What was he like (verse 22)?

6. How did Moses try to help his fellow Israelites (verses 23-29)? Why didn't they respond to his "help"? What happened to Moses?

7. When and how did God appear to Moses again? Contrast Moses, his mission, and the people's response before and after his forty years in the wilderness (verses 35-36). What made the difference?

8. In addition to his leadership of Israel, what other function did Moses fulfill (verse 38)? Instead of waiting for God to fulfill his promises, what did the

people's impatience lead them to do (verses 39-43)? How did God respond to their rejection of his messenger, which was a rejection of him as well?

9. Up to this point in Stephen's message, we have seen people responding to God's messengers with jealousy, lack of understanding, outright rejection, disobedience, impatience, and idolatry. Think of examples of how people today respond in similar ways to Jesus and his message.

10. According to verses 44-50, where did the people worship during their time in the wilderness, during their early years in Canaan, and during the reign of Solomon? Although God was pleased with the places of worship that Moses and Solomon built, where did God say he lives? How do we tend to limit God to manmade buildings today?

11. Read again the charges brought against Stephen in Acts 6:11-14. How had Stephen defended himself by revealing his attitude toward God, toward Moses and the Law, and toward worship in the temple?

12. What charges did Stephen level against the religious leaders of his day (verses 51-53)? In what way was their response to Jesus Christ, God's final messenger, similar to their forefathers' reaction to God's previous messengers?

13. When they accused Stephen of not keeping the Law, what did they not see about their own response to the Law?

14. Why do we all have "blind spots"? How can we learn to see ourselves as God sees us?

PERSECUTION INTENSIFIES

ACTS 7:54–8:25

*U*nfortunately, those in the audience when Stephen spoke preferred their own version of history. His strong words, though true, brought results that may have been surprising to him and the other believers. What followed rocked the new faith community and set its course, one that would eventually divide society in the first century and every century to come.

1. What is the worst persecution you have experienced for your faith?

READ ACTS 7:54–8:1A.

2. What did the council think of Stephen's message? What did they do to Stephen, God's messenger?

How did this prove the truth of Stephen's charge in Acts 7:51-53?

3. What strengthened Stephen during this crisis? Who watched Stephen being martyred, and how did this person feel about these events?

4. Imagine a situation in which Jesus demands a choice of you: You can stand for him and his message, or you can align yourself with those who mock or ignore him and his message. What would determine your choice?

READ ACTS 8:1B-8.

5. What happened in Jerusalem immediately after Stephen's death? How did these events help fulfill the promise of Acts 1:8?

6. What did the scattered believers do?

7. Who was Philip? (See Acts 6:5.) In what ways was his message to the Samaritans confirmed?

8. What changes would be needed for a whole city to have joy (verse 8)? Think about your own town or city. Is it filled with joy? Why or why not?

READ ACTS 8:9-25.

9. What effect did Simon have on the people? Why?

10. Where was Philip's attention focused (verse 12)? Where had Simon's attention been focused (verse 9)?

⌀ 11. What brought Peter and John to Samaria? What
had the people already received (verse 14)? What
did they still need to receive? How did the apostles
help them in this further step of faith (verses 15,17)?

12. Why would Simon have been bitter about what was
happening in Samaria? How could Simon be made
right with God? What still concerned him most
(verse 24)?

13. How do people try to buy the favor and power of
God today? How might this be a problem for you
personally? What is your primary motivation for
following Christ?

AN ETHIOPIAN WHO WAS
READY FOR THE GOSPEL

ACTS 8:26-40

The story has been told of a missionary in Korea who happened to sit on an outdoor bench with an elderly woman one day. They began to talk, and the missionary, sensing the woman's openness, asked if he might tell her about God's Son, Jesus. The old woman's face lit up, and she said that she had always known that God had a son, but this was the first time anyone had told her his name.

Although we know that God has worked in the world since the time of its creation, we are still surprised to discover how miraculously he has prepared people, even cultures to receive the good news of Jesus. In today's passage, one of the disciples experienced firsthand how mysterious are the ways of God.

1. What subject in school was most perplexing to you? Why?

READ ACTS 8:26-40.

Have four volunteers read this section, one person reading the narration, another taking the part of the angel of the Lord and the Spirit of God, and the other two taking the roles of Philip and the eunuch.

2. Review all your information about Philip up to this point. What do you discover about the Ethiopian? Who brought these two men together?

3. What did the Ethiopian need? How could Philip meet that need?

4. Where did Philip begin? What might Philip have included in his "good news" about Jesus?

5. How do we know that the Ethiopian believed the message about Jesus Christ? What did the

Ethiopian and the Samaritans both experience
(verses 8,12,38-39)?

6. Where did Philip go from there, and what did he
do? Who guided his life?

7. What have we learned up to now about Philip's use-
fulness to the Lord? What qualities does God look
for today in people who live for him?

8. Philip performed miracles; Simon practiced magic.
Describe the differences between these men in terms
of their sources of power and the results.

9. Review what you know about the people in Samaria, Simon the magician, and the Ethiopian eunuch (Acts 8). What were they looking for? Whose needs were met in Jesus Christ? What did Simon miss?

10. Have you let Jesus give you what you need? If not, why not respond to him by faith right now? Just say to him, *Lord Jesus, I ask you to come into my life, forgive my sins, and make me your child. Thank you for dying and living for me.* When you trust Jesus Christ, the Holy Spirit comes into your life at that very moment of commitment. He is your guarantee that you truly belong to God. As you yield to him, he gives you the power to live like a child of God.

    If you have just trusted Christ, sign your name and write the date below.

11. Who in your circle of acquaintances needs to understand the gospel? Ask God to give you opportunities to be his "interpreter."

CHANGING LIFE'S DIRECTION

ACTS 9:1-31

*R*enowned author C. S. Lewis once said that he had been dragged "kicking and screaming" into the kingdom of heaven. He didn't mean that God forced him to make a decision. Rather, the overpowering inclination toward the truth and light really left him no other choice but to become a Christian. At another time he wrote, "I believe in Christianity as I believe that the sun has risen, not merely because I have seen it, but because by it I have seen everything else."

Saul of Tarsus, who held the coats of those who stoned Stephen, experienced a similar kind of illumination. He hadn't sought it, but it changed his life and work forever.

1. How did God first get your attention?

READ ACTS 9:1-19A.

2. Check back to when we first met Saul in Acts 7:58 and 8:1. What effect did Stephen's death seem to have on him? What was still his purpose (9:1-2)?

3. By what term was Christianity now identified? Read ahead in Acts 26:9-11 for Saul's statement about the violence of his opposition to Christians. (Saul's name was changed to Paul when he became a follower of Christ.)

4. In what dramatic way did God get Saul's attention? Who had Saul really been persecuting when he harassed the Christians?

5. How did his encounter with Jesus affect Saul physically? How did it affect his traveling companions?

6. Why do you think Jesus chose to meet Saul in such
    a dramatic way? What fact about Jesus was Saul
    forced to recognize, a fact about which the disciples
    had already been convinced? (See Acts 1:3.)

7. How would you describe Ananias?

8. Why did Ananias hesitate to do what God assigned
    him? What reassured him? How did his obedience
    demonstrate his faith?

9. What did the Lord reveal about Saul's destiny?
    What was Saul's attitude as he waited to hear
    from God?

READ ACTS 9:19B-31.

Also read Galatians 1:15-18. It is unclear exactly when Saul left for Arabia. However, shortly after his conversion he went away to spend time alone with God.

10. Contrast Saul in Acts 9:1 with Saul in verses 20-22, and 27.

11. How did Saul describe Jesus to the people (verse 20)? How would his previous knowledge of the Old Testament have been helpful to him?

12. How disturbing was Saul's preaching to the Jews (verses 23-24,29)? How was the Lord's prediction of verse 16 beginning to be fulfilled? In your opinion, why did God's purposes for Saul include suffering?

  13. Who bridged the gap between Saul and the disciples (verse 27)? How was he living out the meaning of his nickname? (See Acts 4:36.)

14. Read the summary statement made about the church in verse 31. Contrast this with Acts 8:1. How successful had the church's enemies been in stamping out Christianity? How can this account encourage Christians today who are persecuted for their faith?

A NEW VISION

ACTS 9:32–10:48

*O*ne of the most excruciating struggles for the church has been against prejudice and racism. It is not a new problem. In today's passage, we see Peter's racial and religious prejudices exposed. With the help of visions and works of the Holy Spirit, this leader of the early church made major adjustments in the way he viewed the world and God's purposes. At the conclusion of his lesson, Peter could well have voiced this prayer that comes to us from a multiracial group in present-day Johannesburg, South Africa:

> In word and deed,
> in loving and caring,
> in sharing and compassion,
> in participation and confrontation;
> Lord, speak your word to us all,
> give us ears to listen
> and willingness to be involved with and for one
>   another
> and a spirit of obedience.

1. When was the first time you became aware of prejudice? How did it make you feel?

READ ACTS 9:32-43.

✏ 2. How did the Lord use Peter in Lydda and Joppa? What was the result of this work of God in both towns?

3. What was Tabitha's reputation? Why was she called "a disciple"?

READ ACTS 10:1-16.

4. Give a brief character sketch of Cornelius (include verse 22).

5. How did God respond to his devotion? What instructions did the Lord have for Cornelius?

6. What was Peter doing when he saw a vision? Why did Peter object to God's command? (The Jewish dietary regulations are given in Deuteronomy 14:3-21.)

7. What new understanding was the Lord giving to Peter? Why was this insight important just then (see verse 28)? How did the Lord drive home the message?

Read Acts 10:17-33.

8. Who sent the vision? Who sent the visitors? How did the Holy Spirit link the two events for Peter?

9. In verses 25-33, we read of the encounter between two unusual men. What evidence can you find that each was open to God, willing to learn from him, and eager to share the truth with others?

10. Can you think of a time when the Lord sent someone to you or arranged circumstances so that your needs were met and the other person also learned more of God's working? If so, share this with the group.

READ ACTS 10:34-48.

11. According to Peter's informal sermon, on what basis does God accept anyone? Who is the focus of Peter's sermon? List the specific facts Peter gives about Jesus Christ.

12. What happened while Peter was preaching? Why were the Jewish believers surprised? What statement in Peter's sermon was proved by the giving of the Holy Spirit at this time?

13. How does the life of Cornelius challenge you? If you are still searching, as Cornelius was, what more do you need from God to become a believer?

GOOD NEWS
FOR ALL

ACTS 11

*I*t appeared to be a normal Baptist church in Atlanta. But the neighborhood began to change from predominantly white to quite racially integrated. The sizable congregation didn't feel comfortable in the neighborhood anymore. In fact, a number of the members moved to another area of town. The time came when the congregation had to decide whether they would move church services to another area, and the issue threatened to tear the church apart. In the end, they did a radical thing: They decided to keep the church right where it was, and they committed themselves to the neighborhood, whatever that neighborhood would turn out to be. Years have passed, but this church is still one of the most progressive churches in town—though it's smaller than before. And its people have paid a price; they have often faced discomfort and insecurity as they have felt out the margins of their faith in a changing context.

This situation has happened many times; perhaps the first time in Acts 11.

1. What have you learned from people who are different from you (culturally, racially, or linguistically) that has enriched your faith?

READ ACTS 11:1-18.

2. Why were some of the Jewish believers in Jerusalem unhappy with Peter? How did he compare what had happened to the Gentiles with their own experience as Jews (verse 15)? What conclusion did he reach (verse 17)?

3. How did the critics respond to Peter's report? Why was the merging of Jews and Gentiles into one church apparently such a crisis issue? (Review Acts 10:28.)

4. What does it mean to you today that redemption through faith in Jesus Christ is not limited to any one group, denomination, nationality, or race?

READ ACTS 11:19-30.

5. What new audience did the scattered believers find (verse 20)? What was their message? What were the results (verse 21)?

6. What objective did Barnabas set for the believers? How was he an example of this goal?

7. Where did Barnabas find additional help for the growing church? What new identifying name was given to the believers in Antioch? What does this term mean?

8. In what practical ways did the Christians in Antioch show their love and concern for other believers? How did each person decide how much to give?

9. Review from Luke's narrative what we have learned about Barnabas. (Read Acts 4:36-37; 9:26-28; and 11:19-30.) Who empowered his life? What were his qualities and motivations?

10. Who has been a Barnabas to you? To whom can you be a Barnabas?

11. What are some of the barriers that keep people from feeling comfortable in your church? What changes could you make to remove some of those barriers?

PETER'S MIRACULOUS ESCAPE

ACTS 12

*G*ive me one hundred preachers who fear nothing but sin, and desire nothing but God, and I care not a straw whether they be clergymen or laymen; such alone will shake the gates of hell and set up the Kingdom of heaven on earth. God does nothing but in answer to prayer." —JOHN WESLEY

1. Think about some of your recent prayer requests. If God answered them, would you be surprised? Explain.

READ ACTS 12:1-19.

2. What were Herod's plans for Peter? How did the church respond to this new crisis?

3. Imagine that you are Peter. You are scheduled for execution the next day. How well are you guarded? How could you sleep so soundly the night before? Who comes to your rescue?

4. What relationship do you think there was between the death of James, the prayers of the believers, and Peter's rescue?

5. Try to sense the humor of the situation when Peter arrived at John Mark's home. What do you think was going through Peter's mind while he waited outside, knocking? How expectant were the Christians that their fervent prayers would be answered? What was their reaction when they actually saw Peter in the flesh?

6. What did Peter share with them? What did he ask them to do? Why? (This James was the brother of Jesus, who had become one of the leaders in the church at Jerusalem.) Before going to a safer place,

why did Peter take the risk of stopping to see the Christians?

7. Why do you think Peter would leave Jerusalem, where the Jews were strong, to go somewhere else?

READ ACTS 12:20-25.

8. Why were the people of Tyre and Sidon worried about Herod's anger toward them? Describe what happened when the representatives of these cities came to see him.

9. What did the people think of Herod? What did God do?

10. What was Luke's analysis of the event?

11. Point out from this chapter how God protects the witness of his Word and the growth of the church even in difficult times. How have you seen the Lord work today in removing obstacles to spreading his Word?

12. Think back over these first twelve chapters of Acts. Luke has told us about the birth, growth, and spread of the early church. What main events stand out in your mind? What individuals made an impression on you? What were some of their problems? What encouraged them?

13. In what ways can we follow the example of these first-century men and women if we want to become Christians (Christ's ones) and if we want the Holy Spirit to move among us as he did among them?

Leader's Notes

STUDY 1: A PROMISED GIFT

Question 2. The kingdom of God (Acts 1:3) refers to the life, death, and resurrection of Jesus Christ and his outreach to the whole world in the preaching of forgiveness of sins. It speaks of the climax of Christ's work in his coming again.

Question 3. For the difficult work ahead (of carrying on the work Christ had begun) "the apostles needed a personal equipment. As the Lord had been baptized with the Spirit and power, so they needed a baptism to make them new men, full of strength, and to enable them to represent the Lord with authority" (R. B. Rackham, *The Acts of the Apostles: An Exposition,* London: Methuen and Co. Ltd., 1912).

Question 4. Acts 1:8 is an outline of what actually happens in the book of Acts. Chapters 1–7 describe the believers' witness in Jerusalem. Acts 8:1–11:18 describes their witness in Judea and Samaria. Acts 11:19-30 describes their witness to the end of the earth.

Question 7. According to Matthew 27:3-10, Judas committed suicide by hanging himself, and the chief priests used the money they had paid him to buy the potter's field. The general interpretation of Acts 1:18-19, then, is that when Judas hanged himself, "his body burst open and all his intestines spilled out." In addition, the "Field of Blood" was bought by the priests in Judas's name since the money was legally his.

Question 8. The practice of casting lots to determine the Lord's will was quite normal in Old Testament days. However, this is the only time the practice is mentioned in the New Testament.

STUDY 2: THE GIFT IS GIVEN

Question 2. Pentecost means "fiftieth" and refers here to the fiftieth day after Passover. Jesus's death and resurrection occurred at Passover time, after which he appeared as the risen Christ for forty days before his ascension. Pentecost was an annual feast day for which many Jews gathered in Jerusalem. This particular Day of Pentecost became the birth date of the Christian church.

Question 3. The baptism of the Spirit, as described in 1 Corinthians 12:13, joins believers with varied racial and social backgrounds into one body, Christ's church. The baptism of the Spirit was initiated at Pentecost. It was later extended to believers in Samaria (Acts 8), to the Gentiles (Acts 10–11), and to the disciples of John the Baptist (Acts 19:1-6). The baptism of the Spirit is received by people today when they believe in Jesus Christ, trusting him as their Lord and Savior. Upon that act of faith, the Holy Spirit comes into the believer's life and unites that person with all other believers as a member of the body of Christ, the church.

Question 7. The phrase "the last days," when used in the Old Testament, referred to the time of the coming of the Messiah (Jesus Christ) and to the accompanying blessings.

In the Old Testament, the Spirit of God usually came upon prophets, priests, and people of prominence. Here, the promise is that the Holy Spirit will be poured upon all God's people, regardless of sex, status, or race. To *prophesy* is to "speak forth" God's words to people.

Question 9. The "day of the Lord" refers to the time at the end of the last days when Christ will come again to establish his kingdom on earth in power and glory.

Study 3: Peter's Plea

Question 7. The gift of the Holy Spirit is dependent not upon water baptism but upon repentance and faith in Christ. Baptism is the outward evidence that an inner change of heart has already taken place. "Baptism in water continued to be the external sign by which individuals who believed the gospel message, repented of their sins and acknowledged Jesus as Lord, were publicly incorporated into the Spirit-baptized fellowship of the new people of God" (F. F. Bruce, *Commentary on the Book of Acts,* Grand Rapids: Eerdmans, 1954, pp. 76-77).

Study 4: Jumping for Joy

Question 4. One of the purposes of miracles in the book of Acts was to authenticate the message of the apostles. Just as the miracles of Jesus attested to his deity while meeting people's deep needs (see Mark 2:1-11), the miracles immediately following his ascension validated the gospel message.

Question 8. The message of the prophets was that God would establish a world kingdom under the rule of Christ, the Messiah.

Question 9. "Most Jews thought that Joshua was this Prophet predicted by Moses (Deuteronomy 18:15). Peter was saying that he was Jesus Christ. Peter wanted to show them that their long-awaited Messiah had come! He and all the apostles were calling the Jewish nation to realize what they had done to their Messiah, to repent, and to believe. From this point on in Acts we see many Jews rejecting the gospel. So the message went also to the Gentiles, many of whom had hearts open to receive Jesus." (*Life Application Bible,* Wheaton, IL: Tyndale, 1988, p. 1624).

Study 5: A Prayer for Boldness

Question 2. This leadership group made up the Sanhedrin, the highest court of the Jews. The Sadducees were a priestly party influential in the Sanhedrin and noted for their denial of the doctrine of the resurrection.

Question 8. The filling of the Holy Spirit should be the normal experience of every believer in Jesus Christ. All believers are indwelt by the Holy Spirit at conversion. We are *filled* with the Spirit as we recognize the sovereignty of God in our lives, express our dependence upon him, ask him to fill us, claim his power to do his will, and walk in obedience to his Word. As the believer yields, the Holy Spirit fills.

Study 6: Sharing Possessions

Question 2. "The early church was able to share possessions and property as a result of the unity brought by the Holy Spirit working in and through the believers' lives. This is different from communism because (1) it was voluntary sharing; (2) it didn't involve *all* private property, but only as much as was needed; (3) it was not a membership requirement in order to be a part of the church. The spiritual unity and generosity of these early believers attracted others to them. This organizational structure is not a biblical command, but it offers vital principles for us to follow" (*Life Application Bible,* p. 1626).

Question 9. Peter did not execute Ananias. His death was a sovereign act of God. Peter was probably as surprised as anyone when, in this instance, God chose to judge sin radically and swiftly.

STUDY 7: GOD'S WORK

Question 8. Although the Sadducees dominated the Sanhedrin, "they could take no such action [killing the apostles] without the support of the Pharisaic members of the court. The Pharisees were in the minority, but they commanded much more popular respect than the Sadducees did..." (*Commentary on the Book of Acts*).

Question 10. Read 1 Peter 3:14-17 and James 1:2-4 for the apostles' perspective on trials and persecution.

STUDY 8: CARING CHRISTIANS

Question 5. The laying on of hands was an Old Testament ceremony. "In the present instance the imposition of apostolic hands formally associated the seven with the twelve as their deputies to discharge a special duty. It did not, of course, impart the gift of the Spirit; the seven were already 'full of the Spirit'" *(Commentary on the Book of Acts).*

Question 9. Stephen obviously presented Jesus as the Messiah. His message apparently included teaching that Jesus was superior to the temple and the Law and even greater than Moses. The Jews considered this blasphemous.

STUDY 9: STEPHEN'S SPEECH

Question 3. "Stephen wasn't really defending himself. Instead he took the offensive, seizing the opportunity to summarize his teaching about Jesus. Stephen was accusing these religious leaders of failing to obey God's laws—the laws they prided themselves in following so meticulously. This was the same accusation Jesus leveled against them. When we witness for Jesus, we don't need to be on the defensive, but instead simply share our faith" *(Life Application Bible,* p. 1631).

Question 10. "Stephen had been accused of speaking against the Temple (Acts 6:13). Although he recognized the importance of the Temple, he knew that it was not more important than God. God is not limited; he doesn't live only in a sanctuary, but wherever hearts of faith are open to receive him. Solomon knew this when he prayed at the dedication of the Temple (2 Chronicles 6:18; Isaiah 66:1-2)" *(Life Application Bible,* p. 1633).

STUDY 10: PERSECUTION INTENSIFIES

Question 10. Bible scholars are divided in their opinions as to whether Simon was a true believer. Some believe he was, but that he was still bound by his past life. Others, because of the events recorded in Acts 8, feel that Simon merely professed faith but lacked an inner reality and only intended to increase his own personal power.

Question 11. "The significance of this event lies in the fact that these people were Samaritans. Here is the first step in which the church burst its Jewish bonds and moved toward a truly world-wide fellowship. The imposition of hands was not necessary for the Samaritans; but it was necessary for the apostles, that they might be fully convinced that God was indeed breaking the barriers of racial prejudice and including these half-breed people within the fellowship of the Church" (*Wycliffe Bible Commentary,* Chicago: Moody, 1962, p. 1139).

STUDY 11: AN ETHIOPIAN WHO WAS READY FOR THE GOSPEL

Question 4. Note that Philip led the Ethiopian to Christ by using Old Testament Scripture. He started with the man's concerns and pointed him to Christ, the fulfillment of Isaiah's prophecies.

STUDY 12: CHANGING LIFE'S DIRECTION

Question 4. "Paul thought he was persecuting heretics, but he was persecuting Jesus himself. Anyone who persecutes believers today is also guilty of persecuting Jesus (see Matthew 25:45), because believers are the body of Christ on earth" (*Life Application Bible,* p. 1639).

Question 13. "It is difficult to change your reputation, and Paul had a terrible reputation with the Christians. But Barnabas, one of the Jewish converts mentioned in Acts 4:36, became the bridge between Paul and the apostles. New Christians especially need sponsors, people who will come alongside, encourage, teach, and introduce them to other believers. Find ways that you can become a Barnabas to new believers" (*Life Application Bible,* p. 1641).

STUDY 13: A NEW VISION

Question 2. "In Joppa, Peter stayed at the home of Simon, a tanner. Tanners made animal hides into leather. It is significant that Peter was at Simon's house, because tanning involved contact with dead animals, and Jewish law considered it an unclean job. Peter was already beginning to break down his prejudice against people and customs that did not adhere to Jewish religious tradition" (*Life Application Bible,* p. 1643).

Question 7. "According to Jewish law certain foods were forbidden (see Leviticus 11). The food laws made it hard for Jews to eat with Gentiles without risking defilement. In fact the Gentiles themselves were often seen as 'unclean.' Peter's vision meant that he was not to look upon the Gentiles as inferior people whom God would not redeem. Before having the vision, Peter would have thought a Gentile Roman officer could not accept Christ. Afterward he understood that he should go with the messengers into a Gentile home and tell Cornelius the Good News of salvation in Jesus Christ" (*Life Application Bible,* p. 1643).

STUDY 14: GOOD NEWS FOR ALL

Question 3. Though God promised throughout the Old Testament that Gentiles would be saved, this was extremely difficult for the Jews to accept. This continued to be a struggle for some throughout the first century.

STUDY 15: PETER'S MIRACULOUS ESCAPE

Question 9. The statement "an angel of the Lord struck him down" is "the regular Old Testament phrase for declaring that the event was a divine judgment whatever the physical cause might have been" (Rackham, *The Acts of the Apostles*).

The Fisherman Bible Studyguide Series—
Get Hooked on Studying God's Word

Old Testament Studies

Genesis

Proverbs

New Testament Studies

Mark

John

Acts 1-12

Acts 13-28

Romans

Philippians

Colossians

James

1, 2, 3 John

Revelation

Women of the Word

Becoming Women of Purpose

Wisdom for Today's Woman

Women Like Us

Women Who Believed God

For more information, visit our Web site: www.waterbrookmultnomah.com

Topical Studies

Building Your House on the Lord

Discipleship

Encouraging Others

The Fruit of the Spirit

Growing Through Life's Challenges

Guidance and God's Will

Higher Ground

Lifestyle Priorities

The Parables of Jesus

Parenting with Purpose and Grace

Prayer

Proverbs & Parables

The Sermon on the Mount

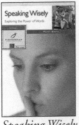

Speaking Wisely

Spiritual Disciplines

Spiritual Gifts

Spiritual Warfare

The Ten Commandments

When Faith Is All You Have

Who Is the Holy Spirit?